AF326891

Blue Woman Dancing in the Nerve

•

Poems by Joan Colby

This book is published as *Alembic* #5. Publication has been made possible by a grant from the Coordinating Council of Literary Magazines, which it made with funds received from the National Endowment for the Arts and from the New York State Council on the Arts.

Most of the poems in this book first appeared in little magazines between 1977 and mid-1979, several in earlier versions. The author thanks the editors of: *Another Chicago Magazine, Blue Unicorn, Buckle, The Cape Rock, Choomia, The Chowder Review, College English, En Passant, Hollins Critic, Images, Manroot, Mid-Atlantic Review, Portland Review, The Shore Review, Spoon River Quarterly, Tinderbox, Unicorn, Uroboros, The Windless Orchard* and *Zahir*.

All poems are divided for pagination between stanzas or sections.

Library of Congress Cataloging in Publication Data

Colby, Joan, 1939—
   Blue woman dancing in the nerve.

   I. Title.
PS3553.04395B55   811'.5'4   79-22754
ISBN 0-934184-01-1 (hardcover) $8.00
ISBN 0-934184-02-X (paperback) $3.50

For my children
Wendelin, Terri, Benjamin

CONTENTS

I

3   Garnet
4   Rosary
6   Vegetable Salad
8   Blood
10   Water-Babies
12   Morning in Late October
13   The Old Nudists
14   The Lady of Flanders — Hypnotic Regression

II

17   The Helper
18   Wet Spring
20   Ah Clio — Muse of History
22   Clio Invents Her Textbook
23   Clio Discourses on Her Shrine
24   Having Tea with Clio
25   Clio Psychotic
26   Clio Takes You as Her Lover

III

29   Owl in the Morning
30   Kisses
32   Octopus Lady
34   Crazy Rain
36   The Language Barrier
38   The Dream That Excludes You
39   The Sleeping Dunes
40   Autumn
41   The Lion's Bride
42   Word Games, Love Games

IV

45   Chiaroscuro
46   White Lilacs
47   Processes
48   Fugue with Two Crows
50   Hospital Poem
52   Blue Woman Dancing in the Nerve
54   Soviets Say Humans Have
        Second Heart — For Lymph
56   Peace

I

GARNET

A darkness
glows in your glass of burgundy.
Shadow eater,
black edged
rose.

Surrounded by a
glitter of nerves
you obstruct the eye—
clot of blood
encrusted in gold.

Semi-precious, abrasive,
enthroned in this elegant setting,
you sit, hematoma,
engorged.

Lady of Wounds
in your menstrual dress,
bless me.

Riding my finger,
Mother Confessor
foretell me,
little cup of blood,
sweet dregs,
dark socket,
solitaire, saturnine,
omen, my
birthstone.

ROSARY

For each bead,
a prayer.
We must have them by heart.

Repetition will beat
down the walls of doubt.
This is the belief.
The walls are wailing walls.

The beads say faith
follows form.
The father comes first.
He is separate.
All his signs proclaim
No Trespassing.

Walking on his grass,
bowing like crazy
we hope he'll forgive us
what we can't help.

A mother is good for that.
There are ten
in a row,
submissive
but with the strength
of quiet voices.
They shine at
interceding for those
who never learn.

Each sits in her window
waiting to aid us.
Every ten
patient mothers
equal one mystery.

There are fifteen altogether.
Only a trinity
could solve them
being a mystery
itself.

It hands out
three separate I.D.'s,
says over and over
"as it is, was
and ever shall be,
world without end."

The father frowns paternally,
keeping a bit detached
from the circle
around whose peripheries
our fingers sneak
searching for that
golden link,
the drowsing archangel
who talks in his sleep.

Will he tell us
where all these
rotations lead
or will he
keep the faith?

VEGETABLE SALAD

CARROT

Orange dagger
guaranteed to curl your hair
and sharpen your eyes,
pulled from a sheath of soil
like the cock of Midas,
gold and stiff,
each bite a new sun sets
between incisors
keeping the hereditary night
blindness at bay.

RADISHES

Red and white as
corpuscles, ·
dwarf politicians
full of the sting of ambition,
tart as a whore's kiss,
pompous as parade soldiers
whose wars are spic and span,
fat as fraus whose hands
are busy with lysol and brushes.

CUCUMBER

Green worm
seeded like the universe,
waxing stout
as a cocoon in which
wonderful changes occur.
Cooling the mouth
like the flesh of warty stars.
Slug, emerald dum-dum
bullet full of good juice.

LETTUCE

Iceberg head,
solid and profound,
level beyond level revealing
a further economy of thought.
To focus is to peel
away distractions
leaf by leaf until the heart is discovered
cold and white, axis
on which all sentiment pivots,
turning rusty at the temples
as an old soothsayer.

TOMATO

Poison heart. Flush with
sleazy glamour
like a slut in a scarlet
rayon wrapper,
eyes a glut of smeared mascara,
lips red and loose
with the telling of forbidden secrets,
buttocks rosy with the juice
of hothouse enterprise.

BLOOD

The scalp blooms
red flowers
in such profusion
cut tongue red
as emperor tulips
vein purpling
like a hedge of fuschias.

Imagine thorns or claws
opening the skin like an envelope
all the red letters falling
in a stream of critical language

or a knife slicing flesh
easily as a jam sandwich.

Think of contusions
how the blood rises
in a million blue helium balloons
to bump against the porous ceiling
turning the sickly greenish yellow
of bad gas.

How the heart, that metropolis,
crams the body's turnpikes
with a constant stream of traffic,
narrow lovers' lanes
luring the maniac
in a pickup black as an embolus.

What legends the blood pursues—
how young girls whisper
of its advent,
how old men sigh when it no longer
gorges in their groins,
how it can be given
to perfect strangers like a bouquet
of long-stemmed roses.

Red animal, how it slinks
through bush-trails,
cut-throat
trout how it lurks in the deep
deltas of the belly. Cardinal
winging like a sudden
hemorrhage from the clotted
bronchial trees.

Examine abrasions as they gush and ooze
with no real damage. Consider
how sometimes the serious wound
is the one that refuses to bleed
closing over its orifice
to breed the deadliest poisons.

WATER-BABIES

My father is reading the story.
Paper birches shiver on the bank.
The dock runs out
plank by plank
to where the water darkens.

The sun capsizes in the lake,
its long glittering wake
pointing like a finger to the shore
where our cottage moors
in a vat of spruce,
a dark and liquid place
beset by sighs.

The harsh roar
of my father's voice
gutters in the quaver
of kerosene lamps.

This story is full of darkness.

I think of the sunfish
swallowing my hook,
its anguished silver flop
desequinning under my knife.

The antique light
flickers in its cage
like a wild bird.

The rafters
hold a wealth of darkness
in their roughened arms
where spiders suspend
and sharp things rustle.
A darkness
that pokes into the snout of every flower,
slipping about the bole of every tree

while the lake grows immense,
a vast black bowl
the night keeps pouring into,
foaming with stars.

I dread
going up to bed alone—
the vigilance of rafters,
the square ogre eyes
of the windows,
the doorknob with its ghastly brass nose.

So I beg for one more chapter
of this story I'm not listening to,
that is over my head,
that will slide
from under my bed,
thick and cold
as a fish
or a monstrous baby
with gill-slits and protuberant
lidless eyes
and bubbles coming from its lips
like words I can't pronounce,
terrors I can't voice.

MORNING IN LATE OCTOBER

The sky is the navy blue
of a schoolgirl's uniform.
Norway maples bugle
golden notes
as wind pushes the stable door
like the calloused hand
of my grandfather. In the loose
box the appaloosa thuds,
wanting grain, the grey colt lips
my hand. My son, small for his 8 years,
bridles the tall chestnut mare.
The smell of urine-soaked straw and manure
infests the aisle where a dim light seeps
through a streaked overhead pane.
At my feet, the dog licks herself.

A cold blast greets us
when we emerge. The fields
are the color of ripe wheat,
the low hills purple. My son,
forked on his mare, leads
the way. I follow ducking
the wind's polished knife,
the bay gelding shuddering
between my thighs.

The road winds
into a sumac thicket
bright as a hemorrhage.
The sky bruises, the maples howl
like a pack of yellow hounds
pursuing the new moon
still hanging in the slate-blue east
like a parenthesis.

THE OLD NUDISTS

Her body is pouchy,
globules of fat pocking
her thighs,
hips like immense sugar bowl handles,
breasts two smashed bags.

He is all wattles
from neck to groin,
his sternum the jutting keel
of a beached ship.

In winter, their house so hot
our minds rock to sleep
watching them waddle. Their familiar heads
spliced to these odious torsos.

We get used
to the faces of the old,
even theorizing the lines
and tortured gauntness
are trophies of coping
but these bodies
seem outrageous, obscene,
decayed yellow sacks
full of wet garbage.

We hug ourselves.
Under our clothes
the loom
of our bones weaves our flesh
into grandparents.

The old man and old woman smile
cordially. They know
what's going on
inside us.

THE LADY OF FLANDERS—
HYPNOTIC REGRESSION

Hands, forming a skein for yarn,
outstretched as though blessing,
now the gown, cloth slippers, veil
over smooth hair, eyes like a calm sea.
I look in the mirror and don't recognize
this woman. Her children laugh and scramble
around my knees. When she was a child
she played in a sunlit road
with some chickens. In a low stone room
she sat at table with her family
supping on dried peas. At seventeen she liked to dance
with garlands of spring flowers.
Her lover peered through a hedge,
his face sullen and dark. His mustache
hung black as a gallows.
Did she marry him? I don't know.
I see her with her children
spinning thread, scrubbing the flagstones.
Her life is utterly content.

She lies in an upstairs room,
the golden ships of morning
sailing through the panes,
her bed linen fluffed like snow.
Her belly is big; the child won't come;
she is dying. Her children ring the bed,
solemn and perturbed. Her hands reach out
without yarn to entice them.
Her spirit refuses to leave. I weep
in the trance. The place is Flanders,
she is 35, the year 1321.

II

THE HELPER

Rolling along behind shafts of light
he dozes while the driver
talks and talks,
the young wife sleeping
in a black contained silence
like the .38 erect along his thigh.

He dreams of the people in the fields
living in lean-tos and the Indians last winter
huddling around an oil drum's
smoky fire. How a woman doublecrossed
by her own arms shuddered
when the wind picked up at sundown.

If he wakes he will see the trucker
steering through a muscular darkness,
the girl curled away,
her hands enclosing the deformity of her face.

He will think himself fortunate
to be hurtling through the dark land
without effort. Tomorrow in Albuquerque
he will help unload.

If he could know that tomorrow
the trucker will be shot from an adjacent stall
as he urinates,
that the young wife will vanish
like the people in the fields
or the Indians in winter,
what could he think about
unless it is the ornate brass
buckle cinching his levis
or the Latigo boots he got
in El Paso last spring.

WET SPRING

The farmhouse settles into its
runaway vines.
The welter of high grass,
overblown lilacs and bridal wreath
exploding in delicate white clusters.
Around back, two women sit
drinking lemonade.
Their faces young, but their bodies
anchored with flesh that moors them
in a life where not much happens.
They talk tirelessly as the wind in the leaves.

Their children play in the junked cars.
One methodically breaks
every window, smashing the jagged glass
into a slush of diamonds.
Another, whose shorts sag from his pot-belly,
staggers crying to his mother,
dead bees stuck to his muddy legs.

She brushes at one absently;
the child wanders off
still howling.
The women's voices drone.

The afternoon prepares its finale.
Black clouds mass in the west,
the sun blurring as the wind chills
from the woodlot raising goose pimples
on the children and the heavy arms
of the women who, still talking,
begin to clear away the empty glasses.
The plastic pitcher falls into the weeds.

The screen door bangs as the first drops
imprint their coin-shapes on the windows.
And behind those windows
the smeared faces of children watch
the rain come down
with a clatter of small change
that goes on and on
like the women talking.

AH CLIO — MUSE OF HISTORY

I am always running across you
in the basement of the
museum of natural history
gnawing dinosaur bones

in the reservoir drinking again

at sea, letting your feet
mingle with salt and water

upstairs dropping the one shoe

in the coal mine letting those braces
fail, the walls caving in (as always
you are saved)

in supermarkets counting your change

the back of your head in every film,
your shadow in every photograph

In the national parks you wear
polaroid sunglasses and drive a
yellow camper

In small towns you lean against
barber-shop windows and spit

I find you
riding first class on Pan-Am

at rock concerts smoking grass
and drinking Ripple

singing to every newborn child

walking all the breakwaters and levees

on observation decks staring
out over all cities, chewing gum

in every Mobil comfort station,
washing your hands.

CLIO INVENTS HER TEXTBOOK

The pages are parchment flayed
from the abdomens of dancing girls.
The spine is made of cartilage
extracted from the knees of senators
which is bound with the sinews
of charwomen and glued
with the bone-marrow jelly
of newborn children.

The covers are of tanned hide
stripped from circus strongmen
and the gilt is from the teeth
of executives. The pages were cut
with the tongues of gossip columnists
and the woodcuts blocked
out of the dreams of virgins.

Now I begin
my story with a pen
that was the forefinger
of a teacher of anthropology
dipped in the blood
of convicted arsonists.

I form the first stroke
which is the shape of a dagger or a pillar,
which can be read as
a numeral or the self's grammatical surrogate.

From here I go on
inscribing everything
in a massive pastiche.

You search these pages
all your life
looking for your fate.

CLIO DISCOURSES ON HER SHRINE

Re: your proposal.
The quarry mentioned
will be fine particularly since
the famous sculptor
prefers it. And the promontory
overlooking
the wine-dark sea
pleases me.

These allusions
are not what I object to:
rather it is the model
you have in mind.
A perfect profile
can never define
my essence.

Thus my instructions:
You may find me
in the deepest
marmoreal vein
a mouth
singing the terrible song
of blood
celled in stone.

Cut me out.

I open and shut,
a red flower,
the raw fist
of your own heart.

HAVING TEA WITH CLIO

Everyone said
you would send the usual
surrogates. All my friends
warned me not to waste
my time. Yet here I am
with the teacups and petits fours,
here with the portraits of Gladstone,
George Washington and Bonaparte,
the busts of Caesar and Socrates,
and this faceless, pendulous breasted,
incredibly ancient big-bellied stone.

I imagine everything that is said
consisting of documents or
famous quotations while the stone
tells riddles within riddles
slyly, as though the meaning
I don't quite get
implies some hilarious
obscenity.

All is not quite lost,
for I'm aware of
you, Clio, incognito
as the prim gentleman in the overcoat
alone at a window table
sipping an imperfect martini,
as the broad waitress
with capped teeth,
as bartender, busboy,
the preoccupied faces
passing down wet streets
in yellow buses that
blunder toward accidents
while
advertising destinations.

CLIO PSYCHOTIC

You undress for blind men and
whisper secrets into the padlocked ears of the deaf.
Clio, your body is the map
of a world that falls away
sharply at the horizon. Touch
the only landfall you honor.
Beyond the stars
your name dissolves like a meteor
encountering the logic of gravity.
Explosions bloom like magenta flowers along the circuits
of your flesh. A solo eye
peers into the cell of mattresses
where you begin to die into otherness.

O Tireless
Stenographer, imagine the pages
you have transcribed anonymously
until nightfall kindles dives and dramshops
to a neon bonfire
where you dance
deliriously in the eyes of lushes
intoxicated with your pretense
of style. Schizophrenic
stripper teasing the boozy masses
you narrow toward daylight
effacing yourself.

Your resume promises lessons
reflecting the future.
The credentials you list
are impressive and useless.
Mad Girl, your eel smile
flickers, a cave of Platonic deceits.
Imagine tomorrow. But backward
glancing's your system.
The trouble we borrow
can never be repaid. You laugh in your sleeve.
Psychopathic liar.
Loving us all for nothing.

CLIO TAKES YOU AS HER LOVER

See how she touches you. This is the way
you've dreamed of being seduced.
Slipping utterly
out of your will into your body.
Her fingers confuse
your sense of origins. All that you tried to know
seems absurd. Let her invent it for you
as she invents pleasure, the spiral nerve
that courses through your flesh,
nightblooming vine,
moon of seven madonnas.

Desire all of her faces. Alecto who never rests,
jealous Megaera, Tisiphone
who avenges . . . winged and snaky women.
Also Aglaie the splendid,
Euphrosyne, giver of joy, Thalie
queen of pleasure. A trinity
of graces.

You kiss her mouth. In the mirror
something flies toward you
like a flock of cranes.
You tremble. The eumenides
are trying on your shadow.
She slides her lithe body
upon yours. You drown in shallows,
phosphorescent water
glitters your eyes like tears.

It's conceivable she talks too much.
Your head whirls over breakfast.
Love defies analysis, you tell her.
She falls silent. Her long nails inscribe
a swastika on your chest. She pastes
a star between your eyes, says
she will burn her diary.

You're in love again. You ask
nothing from her but this:
that you lie all nights in her arms.

She tosses her dice. Snake Eyes.
You win. You lose
yourself entirely.

III

OWL IN THE MORNING

That owl
in the tangle of wild cherry
is hooting again
at sunrise.

Bedded, our elbows and thighs
wrap each other's dream.
Your eyelid
flickers, or is it mine?

All night
on glider wings
he was after the little darting
things in the thickets.

Now he is sated, at home,
his gaslamp eyes burning,
his hooks in the edge
of our minds.

We squirm.
His bald croon
separates day and night,
pulls us one by one
from the country of sleep
to the predatory
truth he repeats.

KISSES

At 13,
a boy stuck his tongue in my
unsuspecting mouth
exploring the roof, gutters of my teeth,
my own tongue dumb
as a rubber mallet.

Soon I became
a kisser whose expertise
scorned passion. Lips and mouth
were not an erogenous zone
like my ears, breasts,
vagina, thighs.

Nevertheless, kissing
is an art in which proficiency
can outpace enthusiasm, so
I used to kiss you for hours
because you like kissing
and I liked doing
what you liked. Months
of kissing! Lips turning on each other
like gears. Oiled. Meshing
perfectly.

But bitter words kept
blooming like rustspots.

Now you're kissing me
with shears.
You think you'll mend the cuts
but they grow deeper,
bleeding.

My lips are razors at your throat.

I hold you even closer.
What else is there?
Kiss me, kiss me where
it hurts.

OCTOPUS LADY

This is my home.
A discarded tin.
I curl in and
disappear.

Seek me. I am
alone. Find me
I become
the color of where I am.

I am a beak
in the middle of myself.
I hesitate
to speak. I am all
arms.

So possessive you writhe
in my coils.
If I must fling myself
suctioning, wrapping
my Rapunzel locks
until you cannot breathe,
forgive me.

A witch-child, I was never taught
the social graces.
The fingercrossed
promises, the little useful words.

Here, beneath my tin hat
I am rapacious
loving you so
I'll suck
you into my core
to distill you from your
self.

When the terrible names men have
given me
erupt from your throat
like gall, remember the
nights I rocked you in so
many arms you moaned,
the dark elastic holes
you rasped in sighing to
find me.

CRAZY RAIN

Twilight.
The dull insanity of rain.

Your mother is telling ghost stories
to the wind. Her words are lost
like indulgences that caused the great split of faith.
You remember for the first time in years
the act of contrition you repeated like a charm
before sleeping. You were a child then
with nothing to be sorry for. The rain
taps the glass, its black fingers
burgling your dreams. It is the stranger
at the door asking directions.
You shoot the bolt. Trust was the first thing
you were missing. Then love saying its name
against the crack in the window.
But it sounded wrong. It sounded
like a scheme. Someone was trying to get in.
You nailed the boards
over those openings. Only the rain
swiveled through the fish-scale roof,
taking the way
of least resistance. Now it draws
a silhouette of loss on the ceiling
over your bed. Those four posts,
the evangelists. You slept in their
care under the guardian wings
of angels plucked
for your comforter.

You're no child any longer.
The child you were
cringes from this sentence and grows small
as a comma.
Each impersonation of the mirror
frightens you. The bone and ash
of your ancestors. The name you sign.
The ghost
in your head who suddenly remembers.

The rain is unfeeling. It pits the earth.
The earth is unfeeling, too.
What are you doing here
expecting to be loved.

It rains, it rains
like crazy.

THE LANGUAGE BARRIER

My grandfather married
a stone, spent
his life carrying it
from one place to another
until he was as bent
as a foothill.

My grandmother slept with the wind.
All her children
were sighs.

This story
is as old as snakes or apples.

Translate this poem.
You'll find a bone with no marrow.

But let me deceive you.
Let me come to you
on a cancelled postcard,
send you bouquets of chicory,
whisper my foreign tongue
in your telephone.
Slip into your dream, a wetback
from the impoverished land
you fly over, sleeping.

Here I am,
a woman; an alien.

We'll come together
chiming the quarter-hour
like expensive clockworks as if
we were made
for each other. Turn
to opposite walls
to dream beyond translation.

I pull the feather quilt up to my ears
looking at the
noose around the moon
that for years and years
has meant bad weather
to everyone.

THE DREAM THAT EXCLUDES YOU

My abdicated name
flashes like an obituary—
you are not the loved one
mourning me. Nor are you the stranger
in the grilled doorway
snapping his fingers at the hips
of passing women. I realize
how silently the velvet sockets
of the body work. It wasn't you
kissing my breasts
with the curtains blowing
away from the stars. Not you
clasping my hand
while the Perseid showers
divulge how everything is falling
apart in a long stream of recurrence,
the trickery of shields or mirrors
that disengage me
from the hiss of my snaky curls.
Not you with the magic bridle
flying to heaven on my body.

THE SLEEPING DUNES

I am the prisoner of sleep.
We are at the dunes again. White sand
burning the soles of our feet
as we climb slipping, seizing a purchase
of dune grass. Beyond, the lake flashes
its blue tambourines.

The dunes slow-dance
the classical figures of change. The lake erodes,
beach houses gradually collapse.
I take your hand. A setter prances
in and out of the breakers, its red pelt
flaming. A beach ball floats
away from the splashing children.
The beautiful wet stones
dry in our hands losing the gleam of riches.
We walk to the blow-out. Dragonflies
stutter their iridescent blue syllables
low over the pools.

We don't need talk.
Glitter of spume, mica,
angular cry of a gull
speaks in our bodies. Says
let everything happen.

An undertow of light tugs our eyes.
Every dream ends with a flooding away.

AUTUMN

The flood gates
moss over,
stone wings stuck
in open flight for years
while the river silted,
swerved and cut
a new channel to the Mississippi.

Birds halt in the elms above
to tell some gossip
we don't dream of. We
hold hands, wild geese
appear in the flyway going south.

Winter gears down
over the hills, its grey piston
cased in cold grease.

Here,
where the Fever River used
to grow delirious,
we sit in a dry bed
choked with milkweed
and the arterial red of sumac,
looking at the curves
that water teaches earth.

The hurts that still distort us
even now, years
since the terrible waters rose.

I watch
the floodgates close
upon your words
and in the hills I hear
dams breaking.

THE LION'S BRIDE

I dream of a lion,
motionless, gold,
its great tawny eyes
glowing, jaw lolling,
as it turns to focus me
in the gemstone of its gaze.

I flee through corridors
while it lopes tirelessly
heading me into the ambush
I've set myself.

Vibrant as the tone of a cello
the muscles interplay
under a layer of plush,
a piston cased in velvet.

Symbol of majesty
and of sloth
it blinks and yawns
as I watch in a spasm
of terror and love.

The book says the lion dream
represents a fate
that must be overcome
if one is to live without fear.

I wake in the pride
of your arms, your topaz eyes blazing
like the risen sun, your sign,
source of all life if kept
at precisely the right distance.

Your hand grazing my breast—
enigmatic, hesitant—
you know how you can hurt me
if I come too close.

WORD GAMES, LOVE GAMES

As we make love
nine red roosters flap
along the ridgepole of my mind
then cock-a-doodling
raggedly rise up
a hodgepodge of randy
red feathers.

Nine comic roosters
instantaneously stuck
upon a wide white sky
as if a match had struck them
into simultaneous outcry.

Picture-book
roosters with lipstick combs
and feisty outlines like
rough-feathered kettles
boiling until they rock
on their hilarious toes
that clutch the high beam
I am becoming
heavy, heavy in your arms.

IV

CHIAROSCURO

The woman wearing white
is a bride on her way to a funeral.
Her hands are ten spines
of an ivory fan. She blesses herself
from a white marble font
supported by angels.
When her eyes roll up exposing the whites
she is fired upon by a thousand candles.
Here is her life: a prayer book
between her palms
inscribed in a dead language;
a rosary of crystal,
each bead capable
of splitting light.
Lilies of the valley are the bouquet
to keep her pure.
Little venomous bells
deadly to the palate.
The woman who wears white
is consumed like a flame in hell.

Although she is a widow
the woman in black says
"I am one whose life is happening
behind every window."
She has learned so much sorrow
that joy is all she'll answer to.
When bats caress the screens
and leaves elongate with darkness
she slips a black lace mantilla
over her smooth dark hair.
The mole between her breasts
glows like a black jewel.
Her whisper slides through the room
with Stygian intrigue. The incense
of her body is a score written in eighth notes.
The woman who wears black
is the rich plum that was bitten.

WHITE LILACS

The white lilac has a hundred ghostly fingers.
It points at the first stars.
It points at me
standing in a May twilight
with barbed wire hooking the darkness where
barbs of stars bloom astonishingly.
                    The cones of the white lilac
shake in a dark wind from the south.
Fragrance rattles
into air, odor of sweet
bones, night-mouths.

All night the lilacs will shudder here
at the edge of the meadow while
stars dazzle the sky's bush.
That black bush of menace.

A ghost
walks over my grave as my flesh rises.
The roots of the lilacs
strive through my skull discovering the holes
I gaze out of. Existence
is terrible. The white lilacs
tremble as I tremble
departing into themselves,
into their clusters of oneness,
refusing to be a symbol,
admitting nothing.

PROCESSES

Ten years ago
I was writing poems
brief as bird tracks.

A wing
encapsuled an entire spring.

Three morning grace notes
scored all summer.

A single beak
bit off autumn like a worm.

A few hieroglyphs
on the snow
said everything there was
to know of winter.

I was younger then.
I was more certain.

All my short spare poems
knotted themselves into a final word
like a crow shot from a tree.

But I've lost that brevity,
that arrogance
of what is what,
and my poems
flock like blackbirds
gleaning word after word,
line after line
from the waving field.

They are still famished,
cawing terribly in my mind.
I don't know what to give them.
I keep on writing
and writing.

FUGUE WITH TWO CROWS

A morning in late winter.
Two crows light on a topmost branch,
unkempt as old trappers,
their black ragbags clutched
like stolen money.

Three months' hard freeze. Today:
a thaw. Further on, the river croons
like a revived baby
beneath its lacy coverlet of ice.

It shakes a rattle of bone.
Abandoned child
of cannibals.

Every roof looses its frozen tear.
So much pent-up feeling,
the snow has grown ancient and grey with it.

The crows
overlook landscape.
Plunderers. Looters.
The windows of ice are cracking on every lake.
The small fish cruising
in gangs learning the sense of grab,
the rule of blood. How the willows
bend into jigsaw water
like native women whose sons wandered off
lured by the river goddess
in her sinuous and fitful bed.

A harsh cry
stabs through the trees'
stupor. The crows
flap off into the sleet
that begins its downfall of needles.
What heavy birds! Sad black hearts!
The hinges of their wings seem to groan
like the rheumatic branches. My eyes
ache with the freight
of their passing.

HOSPITAL POEM

Black shapes sweep the length
of echoing halls. The night
falls from the ceilings in crammed rooms
hissing with oxygen or dreams.

The nurses' station blinks
white as bone. Down the corridor
one voice, after the graveyard
shift arrives, calls
help me   help me
a thin wheedling note
from a distant childhood.

A sigh from the traction bed
rustles the black wool air
like a sandbag full of dead hopes.

An old man dies
begging for ice;
he is given
lukewarm sips and sharp
unshriven warnings not to
disturb. He rattles
the rails all night to the final
throttle jamming his
gobbler throat.

I think of the sign that appears
on the half-closed doors
isolating the cold white ghost,
the pad of the stretcher
borne by grave men
in the hours of the dead
so as not to upset
either cracked ankle or amputation.

The moon rises over the courtyard.
The night is cold, a potion of darkness.
I turn my face to the
window's wound. I should feel old
and bitter but the air
is chilled dry wine
flowing past the dead
tissue of my lungs. A red
flashlight illuminates
terror or pain. But I
am looking the other way watching
the moon lift
on invisible strings that extend
from my body,
from blood, muscle, tendon and bone,
taut and quivering
as each nerve end.

The moonlight silvers
the ancient bricks, pouring into
this small enclosure
like a river, like a river.

The moon is round,
white as a pill.
I swallow it
and sleep forever.

BLUE WOMAN DANCING IN THE NERVE

A blue woman
inhabits the nerve.
She is agitated,
applauds distractedly
for any music, her posture
a coiled spring's curve.

She tap-dances in blue metal shoes,
her hair, electric,
a colony of sparks.
Her eyes two blue revolvers.

Love her, she melts.
Molten lead
in a sleeper's ear.
She can course through your thought
or your dream like an assassin.
You can't win
against her charms.
Those voodoo bones.
Shrunken skulls.
Toss them and chance
takes over.

Ah, what could substitute for pain
if she were not there raising
and lowering her semaphores
in the shapes of hearts and arrows.

If she imagines failure,
you begin to quake with the realization
of a terrible fault
that has always divided you
and you know
the symmetry of your body is only
an illusion, a kind of score
you have been keeping
against yourself.

Bite the suicide capsule.
What can you lose?

Her color engulfs you.
Blues, blues.
The severed head wailing.

SOVIETS SAY HUMANS HAVE
SECOND HEART — FOR LYMPH

This is the secret heart
pumping without our knowledge,
driving white blood
like albino horses
through the ducts of the spine.

It was there all the time,
that hushed organ. Buried beneath
the harp of ribs
where its double shakes exuberant maracas
like a carnival dancer in Rio. It was thought
passive as a Chinese bride
with bound feet. It was thought
fluid moved through it without resistance
as love flows through high-born women.

Wrong. Wrong.
A clatter of white porcelain bells.
A thousand armies have forgotten
how winter defends its cities,
how hunger grows its white blossom
of frost in the belly.

Dr. Anatoly Tsyb says the second heart is
of no less importance than the one
drumming red wolves of blood
over the steppes. The Cossacks have hardly begun
their dance through the bones. The tsar
gazes out the window of the winter palace.
Revolutions will come.

Pravda reports
the discovery has great significance.
Imagine this:
that a way of loving has always existed.

The peasants in their huts huddling on brick stoves
dream its white flowers.
The nobles in their cold
and drafty palaces dance its mazurkas.

Science examines the body
with radioisotopes.
Art examines the body
with dreams.

The hidden heart
singing its lovesong
like a bird in the white birches
of Siberia.

PEACE

(After a painting by Chagall)

The lion woman prances
in a land of kites and stars.
The winged prophet
brings the tablet of laws.

Painted with cuneiform
words of Babylon, the snake
is seeking the flying book.

A woman streaming blood
clutches her infant while her assassin
sings a prayer to his knife.
A child sleeps on a dead bird.

An angel falls in splotches
of red and yellow. The man with a scythe
strides into the village
where children mount birds and vanish.

Christ
is on the cross of the human body.
At his feet hundreds embrace
for the last time.

The naked woman
forgets her dream of love and flowers,
the double-cross of her empty arms.

Above the sun and the moon
the son of god is dying.
The woman with no face

tells all there is of sorrow.
O seven-pointed star!
O lopsided blue heart!

This book was designed and typeset by David Dayton. The poems are set in Tiffany Light with Tiffany Demi titles. The cover is set in Benguiat Bold Condensed Italic; front and back matter, in Benguiat Book Condensed. A first edition of five hundred copies was printed in September 1979 by Ithacaprocess Graphics. Fifty were library sewn and bound into buckram covers and the remainder perfect bound by Page Bindery, also of Ithaca.